# THE *Same* BUT *Different*

*Embracing The Authenticity of God's Creation "ME", "YOU","US"*

Randalle Marie -Cheron Carter

www.TrueVinePublishing.org

The Same But Different
Randalle Marie -Cheron Carter

Published by
True Vine Publishing Co.
810 Dominican Dr.
Nashville, TN 37228
www.TrueVinePublishing.org



Printed in the United States of America—First printing.

# DEDICATION

## To My Spiritual Fathers – Gerard Bagsby & Calvin Lockett

As this book centers on embracing the authenticity of who you are in God, I recognize that this journey is not just about identity, it is about relationship. A relationship with the Father, the One who chose us intentionally and positioned us for such a time as this.

I have come to understand that identity cannot be fully embraced without first encountering the heart of God as Father. And while that revelation is spiritual, God, in His wisdom, often uses people to help us experience Him more deeply.

I could not have cultivated the relational connection I now have with God the Father without the divine guidance, covering, and investment of my spiritual leaders, Pastor Gerard Bagsby and Bishop Calvin Lockett.

Pastor Bagsby was gifted to me and my family during a critical season of development, when the direction of my life was visible, but not yet clear. He instilled in me the discipline of the Word of God and the consistency of intentional time with Him. He taught me that relationship with God is not accidental, it is cultivated through commitment, pursuit, and presence.

Nearly a decade later, God connected me with Bishop Calvin Lockett at a time when that discipline had taken root, but required ignition. What I experienced under his leadership was more than growth, it was awakening. A fire I didn't know I needed. A deeper encounter with the Holy Spirit that shifted me from understanding God to truly experiencing Him.

Who knew that surrender could awaken such fire?

That intimacy with God could set you ablaze in a way that transforms not just how you live, but who you are.

I am deeply grateful for their investment, their wisdom, and their unwavering commitment to their call. But more than anything, I am grateful for their **"yes."**

Their obedience in the natural helped me recognize and receive the covering of God the Father in the spiritual.

Because of their leadership, I have come to know God not just as Creator, but as Father. Not just as distant, but as present. Not just as powerful, but as personal.

And for that, I am forever grateful.

I dedicate this book to both of you with honor, gratitude, and love.

Thank you for helping me experience the Father like never before.

With Love and Purpose,

**Your Spiritual Daughter, Randalle Marie-Cheron Carter**

# FOREWORD

*By Pastor Gerard A. Bagsby*

In a world that often pressures us to conform, compare, or conceal, *The Same But Different* arrives as both a mirror and a lamp, Randalle Marie-Cheron Carter reflecting the truth of who we are while illuminating the sacred intention of God in our uniqueness. This text is not merely a book to be read; it is an invitation to be seen, known, and embraced within the authentic design of our Creator.

From the opening pages, Mrs. Carter gently guides readers into the sacred space where identity, story, and faith intersect. She reminds us that the journey toward wholeness often begins with honest reflection: "my story, your mirror." In doing so, she affirms a profound theological truth, that each life, shaped by unique experiences and contexts, still bears the unmistakable imprint of being made in the image of God.

We are, indeed, the same in origin and worth, yet beautifully different in expression and calling. What makes this book especially compelling is its compassionate exploration of tension: nature and nurture, belonging and exclusion, fracture and wholeness, individuality and community. Mrs. Carter does not approach these themes with abstraction but with lived awareness. She understands that identity is not formed in isolation but within relationships: family, culture, church, and society. Where those systems nurture, we flourish; where they wound, we fracture. Yet her message never leaves us fragmented. Instead, she consistently points us toward restoration through Kingdom connection and community.

Chapters such as When Belonging Breaks Down and Building Kingdom Community are particularly timely for the Church today. They call believers beyond surface-level unity toward a deeper, Spirit-formed communion that honors both shared identity in Christ and the God-given distinctiveness of every person.

Carter's vision of community is not uniformity but harmony, a consecrated chorus of voices, testimonies, cultures, and callings joined in worshipful purpose. At its heart, *The Same But Different* proclaims a liberating declaration: authenticity is not  rebellion against God's design; it is the embrace of it. To accept the truth of "me," "you," and "us" is to honor the Creator whose image we carry. This message speaks prophetically into an age struggling with identity, belonging, and worth.

It is my prayer that every reader experience in these pages both affirmation and awakening: affirmation of how much they're loved by God, their inherent worth and an awakening to the beauty of others. May this book stir deeper compassion, courageous self-acceptance, and renewed commitment to building Kingdom communities where all God's children are welcomed as they were divinely created: the same in sacred origin, yet wonderfully different in expression.

—Pastor Gerard A. Bagsby

Capacity is defined as the ability to receive or contain; the power of receiving impressions, knowledge, and mental ability. Capacity is often the overlooked quality that allows individuals to achieve comprehensive success while navigating multiple roles. If the word capacity needed a poster child, Elder Randalle Carter would be the leading candidate. She is a field grade officer in the military, an elder in the Lord's church, a wife, mother, CEO of a nonprofit, and a community leader. The grace on her life allows her to juggle many responsibilities without dropping any.

One of the attributes I admire most about Randalle is her consistency. I met her during a Bible study nearly three years ago, and since that time, her consistency has been unparalleled. Randalle's testimony is simple: she shows up; not just for me, my family, or our ministry, but for countless others around the country. I've watched her work on a Friday, fly out Friday evening to another state, and return Saturday night, all to be present for church Sunday morning just to support someone she loved or someone in need. Her consistency has allowed me to build and invest a deep level of trust in her that continues to grow. Quite candidly, "Randie" is one of the most consistent individuals I've encountered in my entire life.

Randalle's literary masterpiece, *The Same But Different*, encourages us to embrace the wonderful individual God created each of us to be. Far too many people can see the beauty in others without appreciating the reflection they see each time they look in the mirror. Like Barnabas, Randalle possesses "the spirit of encouragement." After reading this book, you will be motivated to acknowledge the amazing and authentic characteristics that distinguish you from everyone else on the planet. She masterfully demonstrates that each of us is "…fearfully and wonderfully made…" (Psalm 139:14).

Now, turn the page and expand your intellectual capacity by reading this amazing book. You'll be so glad that you did!

**Bishop Calvin B. Lockett**
Founding Pastor
Christ the Healer Church
Clarksville, Tennessee

# Table of Contents

# Chapter 1

## THE STARTING PLACE –
## MY STORY, YOUR MIRROR

**N**ever in a million years would I have imagined that my life would be where it is today.

Do you ever think that to yourself?

Maybe the thought rises in moments of gratitude, when life feels steady and full.

Or maybe it comes in moments of grief, when you're forced to confront what didn't unfold the way you hoped. Either way, that thought eventually finds all of us.

No matter where we are in life, reflection is unavoidable. And for me, reflection always leads to the same question:

### Where do I even start?

Do you ever feel that way about your life? About the responsibilities that fill your days. About the version of yourself you're trying to become. I wish I could say there's a manual. A clean, step-by-step guide to beginning again. But there isn't. As disciplined as I may appear after 21 years in the Army, I still wrestled with starting.

Mornings are the hardest. Not because the day is heavy, but because sometimes it feels like the night never truly ended. When rest is incomplete, the start feels misaligned, and when the start is off, everything else follows like falling dominoes.

Routine has shaped my life. Physical fitness is as natural to my morning as brushing my teeth. But I've noticed something: brushing my teeth requires far less effort than completing a workout. Isn't that true in so many areas of our lives? We gravitate toward what costs less.

If we're honest, we often choose the path of least resistance, not because it's right, but because discomfort feels unnecessary. Yet Scripture reminds us: "Let us run with endurance the race that is set before us." — **Hebrews 12:1**

Endurance implies discomfort. Growth requires stretching. Transformation demands resistance. The problem is not that we don't want growth. It's that we don't always want the discomfort that precedes it, and sometimes the reason we don't grow is because we don't truly understand where our real starting place is.

## Let me introduce you to Jacob.

Jacob's story begins with tension. Even before birth, he was grasping his brother's heel (Genesis 25:26). His name literally meant *"supplanter"* or *"deceiver."* His natural start was marked by rivalry, insecurity, and self-reliance.

Jacob manipulated his way into securing Esau's birthright (Genesis 25:29–34). He deceived his father Isaac to obtain the blessing (Genesis 27). For years, Jacob relied on his intelligence, strategy, and calculation to build his future. He did not trust God to secure what God had already promised. Jacob's natural starting point was self-preservation. But his true beginning didn't happen at birth. It happened at Peniel.

In Genesis 32:24–28, Jacob wrestles with a Man through the night. Scripture says: "So Jacob was left alone, and a Man wrestled with him till daybreak." — **Genesis 32:24**

He refused to let go until he received a blessing. Even after his hip was dislocated, he held on, and then came the shift.

"Your name will no longer be Jacob, but Israel, because you have struggled with God and with humans and have overcome." — **Genesis 32:28**

## Jacob walked away with two things:

- A new name
- A permanent limp

The limp represented weakness. The name represented transformation. His start was not his birth. His start was his surrender. Jacob's true beginning came when he stopped striving and started depending, and maybe that's true for us too. We often think our beginning is our family background, our last name, our trauma, our failures, or our reputation. But Scripture says: "Therefore, if anyone is in Christ, he is a new

creation. The old has passed away; behold, the new has come."
— **2 Corinthians 5:17**

Our real start is spiritual, not biological.

## So now, let me introduce myself.

My name is **Randalle Marie Cheron Carter**, and at 42, I feel like I am just beginning the life God always intended for me. I recently retired from the Army after 21 years of active-duty service. I am a wife of 14 years. I am a mother of three beautiful daughters. A founder of a nonprofit organization focused on financial literacy, educational enrichment, youth entrepreneurship, and cultural empowerment.

None of these were in my original "starting plan", but God had a different one. Growth didn't come overnight. It came through brokenness, through surrender, and rediscovering who I was, not just as a woman, but as God's creation.

God means many things to many people. To some, He is distant. To others, He is a judge, a mystery, an afterthought, but to me, God is the One who connected the dots when I couldn't see the picture. He showed up emotionally, spiritually, and mentally when I didn't know how to show up for myself.

Psalm 139:16 says: "Your eyes saw my unformed body; all the days ordained for me were written in your book before one of them came to be."

That means my beginning was written before I understood it. So was yours.I didn't always live with that clarity. Like Jacob, I wrestled. I tried to control outcomes. I feared surrender because surrender meant loss of control.

But what I didn't understand was this: The pressure felt unbearable because I believed I had to carry it alone. I had not yet embraced that God equips those He calls (Hebrews 13:21). He prepares us as we walk toward the beginning He already designed. And slowly, through tension, through mistakes, through quiet surrender, I began to recognize something: God's hand was there from the start, guiding, shielding, shaping, and protecting me, even when I didn't recognize Him.

So let me ask you:

## What's your story?

Everyone has one. Spoken or silent, it shapes how we love, trust, protect, and show up in the world. Mine includes young parents divorced shortly after I was born. Questions about identity before I had language for them. I often wondered, Who am I when the people who created me are no longer together? Would my life be different if my start were different?

But here's what I now know: Momentum does not dictate destiny. Your beginning does not disqualify you from purpose. God forms identity in the middle of unfinished stories.

This book is not about blaming the past. It's about redefining your starting place. We must refuse to be afraid to start. Because your beginning is not defined by your birth. It is defined by your surrender.

Like Jacob, your new name awaits on the other side of wrestling, and only you can delay what God has already designed. It starts with you, and it starts with God.

# Chapter 1 Reflection Questions

## "The Starting Place"

1. When you think about your life, what do you consider your "starting place"? Is it your family, your failures, your achievements or your surrender to God?

2. In what ways have you been operating from self-reliance like Jacob before Peniel? What would surrender look like for you?

3. What discomfort have you been avoiding that may actually be the doorway to growth? (Hebrews 12:1)

4. How has your family origin shaped your identity? Where might God be inviting you to redefine that starting point?

5. If God were to "rename" you spiritually today, what identity would He call forward in you?

6. What area of your life requires a new beginning, not because your past was wrong, but because your dependence needs to deepen?

7. Do you lean in or hesitate out of fear, doubt, or inadequacy?

8. What role has God played in shaping your journey so far, even in the moments you didn't recognize His hand?

9.  If you could define your "starting point" with God today, what would that look like? What would you leave behind to embrace what He's calling you toward?

# Chapter 2

## MADE IN HIS IMAGE

"In the beginning, God created the heavens and the earth…"(Gen 1:1)

These are the first words of Scripture. Before man and woman ever took their first breath, God was already forming something beautiful: a world, a system, a place of provision. He created light, sky, land, vegetation, animals, waters, and everything in between, and then, He made us—humankind—in His own image.

That truth alone is transformative. Before placing us in the world, God *prepared* the world for us. He created the resources, the rhythms, and the relationships that would sustain us. This is more than just divine planning, it's divine care. God knew we couldn't thrive in a place that had no structure, nourishment, or companionship. So, He made provision first, and then He gave us purpose.

Sometimes we forget that. We forget that before the chaos, before the fall, there was care. That before the confusion of identity, there was clarity: "Let Us make man in Our image, according to Our likeness" (Genesis 1:26). From the very beginning, our identity was rooted in likeness to the Creator. Not in perfection, but in reflection. We were made to mirror Him.

But life has a way of distorting the mirror. When I look at myself in the mirror, I sometimes see bits and pieces of my parents, my siblings, or close friends who have walked with me through many seasons, and that makes sense. The longer we spend in close proximity to someone, the more we take on parts of them just as they take on parts of us. That's the power of shared space.

But what happens when the reflection we see doesn't look like God anymore? The author and finisher of our faith. Is it possible for someone to take the pen and write in His place? What happens when distance from Him causes us to pick up pieces of people or patterns that don't reflect His image at all?

The truth is, it's a lot like our earthly relationships. If I stop spending time with someone I was once close to, I naturally begin to lose the influence they had on me. Their words fade. Their way of thinking no longer shapes mine. Their presence no longer carries weight in my daily life.

It's no different with God. The more distant we grow from Him, the harder it becomes to remember who we are in Him. We start to forget the compassion, the confidence, the peace, and the power we carry, not because we lost them, but because we drifted from the One who gave them to us. We start shaping our identity around what's culturally acceptable, emotionally comfortable, or socially convenient... instead of what's spiritually true.

But here's the beautiful thing: our image-bearing doesn't depend on how perfect we are, it depends on how present we are with Him.

God never withdrew His image from us. It's still there. But clarity comes when we return to the mirror of His Word, the presence of His Spirit, and the rhythm of relationship with Him. We were created to reflect Him, and the closer we get to Him, the clearer that reflection becomes.

For the first twelve years of my life, my relationship with my father was limited to periodic visits when he came to see the family in Texas. I remember the excitement I felt whenever he arrived. It was joy, hope, and curiosity all wrapped in one, but beneath that excitement was also a longing, a deep, unspoken desire to be with him more consistently. I wanted to know what made him laugh, what he valued, and what made him uniquely *him*. I wanted him to know me too; what I liked, what I dreamed of, and how I saw the world. More than anything, I wanted to build memories not just from moments, but from presence.

When I turned thirteen, that desire pushed me to pursue more from our relationship, and to my surprise and joy, he embraced it fully. We became incredibly close, best friends even. We'd talk three or four times a day about everything and nothing. As our connection deepened, others began to notice something different about me. "You sound just like your dad," they would say. "You move like him. You even talk with his preacher voice."

I hadn't changed intentionally, but something *was* changing. Simply being in his presence, hearing his voice, and knowing his thoughts started to influence me. His characteristics, mannerisms, and even his way of seeing the world began to surface in me. The truth is, they had always been there; dormant, maybe, but present. It just took *connection* to awaken the resemblance.

Isn't that exactly how it is with God? Scripture tells us that we were created in His image and likeness (Genesis 1:26). That means there is something of Him already embedded in who we are. His nature. His essence. His character, but the longer we live outside of His presence, the more dormant those parts of us become. The reflection begins to blur. Our image, the one He intended to bear His signature, starts to reflect everything else but Him.

People may still see us. But will they see *Him* in us? When I lacked consistent relationship with my earthly father, there was little to reflect back to the world that connected me to him. But once I drew near to him, the evidence became undeniable. The same is true for our heavenly Father. The closer we draw to Him through prayer, worship, and surrender, the more our lives begin to reflect His image. Not just in words or outward behavior, but in posture, in presence, and in how we show up in the world.

We become more patient, more compassionate, more loving, more resilient. Not because we are forcing ourselves to be good, but because we are *becoming* what we were always created to be—His reflection.

This is why our time with God is so important. It's not a checklist item for the spiritual elite. It's the very environment where our true identity is revealed and cultivated. You cannot reflect what you haven't beheld.

So many of us are walking around spiritually disconnected, searching for clarity, direction, purpose, when what we really need is proximity. We don't need to do more. We need to be *with* Him more.

When you spend time with God, you begin to sound like Him, think like Him,  move like Him, and love like Him. You start to reflect not just a better version of yourself, but the divine nature that He placed inside you from the beginning.

You were made in His image. The question is: Do you look like Him? if not, are you willing to draw closer so that reflection becomes  unmistakable?

# Chapter 2 Reflection Questions:
## "Made In His Image"

Think about a time when you felt closest to God. What was different about your thoughts, your actions, or even your confidence in who you were?

**Now reflect:**

1. When you look in the mirror, who do you see?

2. Who has influenced your identity the most in recent years?

3. What parts of you have become blurry or distant from Him?

4. What would it look like for you to draw closer to God in this season?

Take a moment to write a prayer or declaration inviting God to help you see yourself more clearly through *His* eyes and to reflect Him more intentionally in your daily walk.

____________________________________________

____________________________________________

____________________________________________

____________________________________________

____________________________________________

# Chapter 3

## NATURE VS. NURTURE: THE HUMAN DILEMMA

"Nature vs. Nurture." It's a phrase we often use to explain why people are the way they are. Were you born this way, or were you shaped by your environment? It's a conversation that can open the door for healing, but it can also become a hiding place, a way to avoid taking ownership of where we are and who we've become.

Yes, it's true: many of us were born into brokenness. Some came from homes where love was inconsistent, where provision was limited, and where emotional safety was rarely available. In those spaces, you don't just lack material resources, you lack the *nurture* that teaches you how to build something different when it's your turn. You enter adulthood repeating what you were exposed to, not because you wanted to, but because it was all you knew.

But it's also true that some people defy that narrative.

Some people rise out of the same kind of dysfunction and make a conscious decision to break the cycle. Not because it was easy or because they had all the tools, but because *they chose to.* They chose to want better, to pursue better, to *become* better, even if that meant fumbling through the process.

That's the part we don't talk about enough: *choice.* The lie we often believe is that we are products of our past with no power to change our future, but that's not truth, and it's certainly not Scripture.

Deuteronomy 30:19 says, *"I have set before you life and death, blessings and curses. Now choose life, so that you and your children may live."*

God gives us the ability—and the responsibility—to choose. Not just once, but daily. When we say, "Well, I am the way I am because of how I was raised," what we're often saying is, "I've stopped growing." But when we realize that even our upbringing doesn't have to define our becoming, we move from blame to breakthrough.

The truth is, even if we didn't receive the nurture we needed, we are still made in God's image, and within that divine image lies the power to rise, to shift, think differently, live differently, and choose differently. What separates those who repeat generational patterns from those who break them is rarely circumstance is decision.

Let's look at two biblical figures who made life-altering decisions, though they came from very different beginnings.

First, the woman with the issue of blood. We don't know her name. We don't know her background. Her story enters

Scripture not at the height of her life, but in the middle of her suffering. For twelve years, she endured chronic bleeding, rendering her unclean by cultural standards, isolated from community, and financially depleted from spending all she had on unsuccessful treatments.

Matthew 9:20–22 (NIV) tells us:

"Just then a woman who had been subject to bleeding for twelve years came up behind him and touched the edge of his cloak. She said to herself, 'If I only touch his cloak, I will be healed.' Jesus turned and saw her. 'Take heart, daughter,' he said, 'your faith has healed you.' And the woman was healed at that moment."

Her story is powerful not just because of the healing, but because of the *pursuit* of wholeness. She didn't wait for circumstances to change. She didn't accept suffering as her identity. She made a decision: *If I can just touch Him, I will be healed.*

That kind of faith, the kind that pushes through crowds, rejection, shame, and fatigue, is what transforms lives. It's easy to function in dysfunction because it becomes familiar, but wholeness requires pursuit. It demands effort. It asks us to choose something better than what we've accepted as normal.

This woman knew that her identity was greater than her circumstance. She chose to believe that healing was possible, and she placed her faith in the only One who could restore her.

Now, let's look at Saul, who would later become Paul. Unlike the woman with the issue of blood, Saul entered the biblical narrative from a place of religious status and cultural reverence. He was a devout Jew from Tarsus, educated under the respected teacher Gamaliel (Acts 22:3), and a strict observer of Jewish law. His zeal for preserving Jewish tradition led him to violently persecute early Christians.

But in Acts 9, everything changed:

"As he neared Damascus on his journey, suddenly a light from heaven flashed around him. He fell to the ground and heard a voice say to him, 'Saul, Saul, why do you persecute me?' 'Who are you, Lord?' Saul asked. 'I am Jesus, whom you are persecuting,' he replied." (Acts 9:3–5, NIV)

This encounter with Christ blinded Saul for three days, giving him time to wrestle with everything he believed. Though God initiated the encounter, Saul still had a choice. He could have clung to the identity he had built for himself: an educated man, powerful, respected, feared. Or he could surrender to the new identity being offered to him by Christ. He chose the latter, and the result was a complete transformation. Saul became Paul, a man who would go on to write most of the New Testament and spread the Gospel to the Gentiles.

The contrast between these two stories is striking: one begins with suffering and obscurity: the other with status and certainty. But they converge at the same place: *a decision to pursue Jesus.*

That's the key. Whether your life started in pain or privilege, in lack or abundance, you still get to choose. If your path isn't aligned with God's purpose, there's still time to change direction.

I used to think that the weight I carried in life was mine to bear because of how I was raised, or because I didn't have the tools others had. I've since realized that even if I didn't choose where I started, I am responsible for where I go from here.

Sometimes, we think it's noble to carry the burdens of everyone else, to be the strong one, the connector, the reconciler. For much of my life, I did just that. I filled my space with people's pain, thinking I was helping. But the Holy Spirit revealed something powerful to me: not every burden is an assignment.

Some of the weight I carried was rooted in nurture, how I was raised to survive, to care, to fix. God never intended for those instincts to override His voice in my life. I had to choose. I had to make space for help, for healing; for Him.

That doesn't mean it's easy. It doesn't mean there won't be setbacks. But refusing to choose is, in itself, a choice. That choice often keeps us stuck in cycles of pain, poverty, or passivity that God never intended for us to live in.

Most stories of purpose are born out of pain. It's the fire of disappointment that sparks the desire for something more. It's the grief of a lost childhood that births the passion to give your children better. It's the struggle with insecurity that leads you to discover your identity in Christ. These stories are real, and they're powerful. But more than anything, they're proof that transformation is possible.

The good news of the Gospel is not just that we were created in God's image, but that we can be *reborn* in it. John

3:3 reminds us that to truly see the Kingdom of God, we must be *born again*. That doesn't mean we get a new history, it means we get a new identity. One rooted in Christ, not in chaos. One formed by faith, not just family. One that chooses life, even when everything around us has been shaped by death.

So maybe you were raised in dysfunction. Maybe you didn't have nurturing parents, access to quality education, or the emotional stability needed to thrive. Maybe you were constantly in survival mode, trying to make it from one day to the next, with little hope that things would ever change. But here's the hard truth and the holy truth: you still get to choose.

You still get to choose how you respond to what you inherited. You still get to choose how you show up for your children, your relationships, and yourself. You still get to choose whether you repeat the patterns, or break them.

I don't think I fully understood the magnitude of that power within me until just a few years ago. For most of my life, I have been a connector—a bridge between broken family members, distant friends, and wounded colleagues. I've always had a heart for reconciliation and restoration. I could see potential in people even when they couldn't see it in themselves. I knew how to hold space for pain, and I knew how to love people through their storms.

What I didn't understand, however, was *why* I was always the one in that position. Why it seemed to be *my responsibility* to carry the emotional weight of others. Why it was always *me* leading the charge in moments of reconnection and reconciliation. I told myself it was my calling. That I was simply doing the work of the Lord, and in many ways, I was. But over time, it became exhausting.

There came a moment when I found myself in tears, completely drained from carrying the pain of those around me. I wasn't just interceding for others. I was *carrying* them. Their brokenness, their choices, their emotional residue. In that raw, vulnerable moment, I cried out to God. "Why does this always fall on me? Why do I always have to be the one helping everyone else? Who's going to help *me*?"

And then, in His gentle but convicting way, the Holy Spirit revealed something I'll never forget: "A lot of what you carry wasn't assigned to you. You picked it up out of habit, not out of obedience."

That revelation hit me deep. He showed me that much of what I considered ministry was actually me operating out of a *nurtured pattern*, not a *Kingdom assignment*. I had been conditioned through my upbringing, my environment, and my past, to believe that my value was in *fixing* things, in *being there* for everyone else, in *showing up* even when I had nothing left to give.

That wasn't obedience. That was overcompensation. God made it clear: "I can't send you help when you've filled your space with things I never called you to carry."

Whew. That moment freed me. I realized that the nurturing I received, though well-intended, had trained me to operate in ways that were not always healthy. I was so used to being the strong one, the dependable one, the glue, that I didn't know how to *receive* help. I didn't know how to say "no" without guilt. I didn't know how to leave space for God to step in, because I had already filled it with everyone else's needs.

This is the tension between Nature and Nurture. Your *nature* is the image of God imprinted on your soul; the divine reflection that longs to live in alignment with His purpose. Your *nurture* is the environment that shaped your understanding of love, worth, responsibility, and identity.

When these two come into conflict, it creates confusion. We begin to question who we are, not because our nature is flawed, but because our nurture was incomplete or imbalanced.

But here's the hope: you can choose to unlearn what no longer serves you. You can choose to lay down what God never asked you to carry. You can choose to rebuild your life, not on broken cycles, but on biblical truth.

God gave us free will not so we could be reckless, but so we could *reclaim*. You are not bound by how you were raised. You are not sentenced to repeat what you saw growing up. Even if dysfunction was all you knew, *transformation is still possible*. But it starts with surrender: Surrendering the pressure. Surrendering the false responsibility. Surrendering the nurtured patterns that were never part of your divine nature.

The human dilemma is this: we often don't know how to let go of what raised us, even when it's hurting us. But the

God-given solution is this: He'll teach you how to release it, if you're willing to return to Him.

You can choose life. You can choose wholeness. You can choose to break cycles and build new ones. You can choose to believe that your pain has a purpose, and your identity is not limited to where you came from but anchored in who you were created to be.

# Chapter 3 Reflection Questions:
## The Power to Choose

1. What choices have you made recently that reflect your identity in Christ? Are there any choices you've made out of fear, pain, or survival that you now see differently?

2. Do you identify more with the woman with the issue of blood or with Saul/Paul? Why? How does your journey resemble either of their stories?

3. What "norms" in your life have you accepted that may be rooted in brokenness or dysfunction? Are you willing to pursue wholeness, even if it means leaving familiar patterns?

4. Have you ever mistaken emotional responsibility for a spiritual assignment? What burdens are you carrying that God may be asking you to release?

5. What would it look like today for you to reach for the hem of Jesus' garment? What is one step you can take toward healing, growth, or surrender?

6. What fears have kept you from making a necessary decision to shift your life's direction? How can you begin to walk in the courage that God equips those He calls?

7. In what ways has God been guiding you—even when you didn't see it clearly at the time? Can you identify moments in your past that now look like divine intervention?

8. What space do you need to make in your life right now so that God can send the help you've been praying for?

# Chapter 4

## WHOLE OR FRACTURED –
## WHO GETS TO DECIDE?

What does it mean to be *whole*, and what does it mean to be *fractured*?

These words are tossed around so casually in our culture: self-help books, therapy sessions, even sermons. Everyone seems to have a definition, but when we strip away the noise and the pressure, the question remains: Who gets to decide?

Society would have us believe that wholeness comes through status, success, a healed childhood, or perfectly balanced emotions. If you fall short in any of these areas, if your story includes trauma, instability, or failure, you're labeled as broken, incomplete, or not enough. It's as if the world holds the measuring stick for our worth, waving it over our lives and deciding which parts of us qualify as whole.

But I have to ask: Why does the world get to decide?

If God created us, if He formed us with intention, breathed life into us, and called us "very good," then shouldn't He be the One who defines what wholeness looks like?

Many of us have unknowingly accepted the world's distorted definition of what it means to be whole. In a fallen world, brokenness is inevitably woven into the fabric of our experiences from the moment we take our first breath. We've come to equate wholeness with perfection, healing with performance, and value with validation. That's not how God sees it.

From the very beginning, humanity has carried the weight of a fractured world—one marred by sin, separation, and struggle. Yet, even in that brokenness, God never stopped calling us His own. He doesn't wait for us to "get it all together" before He draws near. He doesn't require perfection before extending purpose. In fact, it's often through our deepest fractures that He reveals the fullness of His grace.

Being fractured doesn't disqualify you, it simply confirms that you live in a world that was never meant to define you.

Being whole doesn't mean you're flawless, it means you're surrendered. It means you've set your heart on becoming all that Christ has called you to be, even in the face of struggle.

Wholeness in Christ is not the absence of weakness; it's the presence of redemption. It's the ongoing, Spirit-led process of allowing God to take every piece of your story, your wounds, your regrets, your fears, and align them with His purpose.

God is not intimidated by your broken places. He formed you fully aware of every flaw, every insecurity, and every hard chapter. He knew the world would fracture parts of you, and He also knew His Son would be the way to restore what was broken.

So, before we go any further, take a breath and ask yourself:

- Whose definition of "whole" have I been living by?
- Am I willing to allow Christ—the One who made me—to redefine what wholeness really means?

Because in the Kingdom, to be whole is not to be perfect. It's to be healed, known, and transformed by the One who never stopped pursuing you.

My grandparents had my mother later in life. Both of them were in their forties. My grandmother had six children before my mom, and my mom was part of the third set for my grandmother and first set for my grandfather. By the time I came along, the complexity of our family structure was already deeply rooted. My grandfather had remarried, and his new wife had children older than my mother. They were technically her "stepsiblings," but old enough to be something entirely different in terms of dynamic.

To the outside world, our family looked fractured. But on the inside, we didn't necessarily have that language, we simply *existed* in what we knew. The idea of "wholeness" didn't come from a textbook definition. It came from moments of laughter in the kitchen, shared meals, family gatherings, and inside jokes that only made sense to us. But still, there were cracks in the foundation. And those cracks had consequences.

The blendedness of our family wasn't intentional, it was the result of circumstances. But it carried consequences just the same. There were wounds we didn't talk about, hurts that never fully healed, and comparisons that cut deeper than they should have.

Some of those wounds were tragic, family molestation that went unaddressed, buried beneath shame and silence. Other wounds came from the sting of perceived favoritism, when those who were not blood received care, affection, or opportunity in ways some of us never did. We saw it. We felt it, and even if it wasn't intentional, it left marks.

Here's the hardest part: *you never truly know the heart of a man or woman's intent.* You don't always know what they were thinking, why they made the choices they did, or who they were trying to protect. That's the complexity of family, it's a mixture of love and loyalty, silence and sacrifice, memory and misunderstanding.

Fractured structures persist not always because of malice, but because of *a lack of conversation.* A lack of acknowledgment. A lack of willingness to say, "That happened. It hurt, and it mattered."

When conversations are avoided, pain festers. When attempts at covering both "blood" and "bonus" family are made without wisdom or openness, someone always gets left out in the cold.

God never designed family to be a place of confusion or comparison. From the beginning, family was supposed to reflect unity, covering, and love. But sin, shame, and silence disrupted that design. We've been trying to find our way back to wholeness ever since.

Even in Scripture, we see fractured families. Think of Joseph, sold by his brothers out of jealousy. Think of David's household, torn by favoritism, violence, and silence. The Bible never hides brokenness, it highlights it, not to glorify dysfunction, but to point us toward redemption.

What I've come to understand is this: the ache to belong is universal. Whether blended, broken, or blood-related, we all long to feel chosen, safe, and known. That's not just a family issue, it's a human issue. It's one that only the Father can truly heal.

In a fractured family, we may not get the apology we hoped for. We may never fully understand why things were the way they were. But we can choose to break the silence. We can choose to name what hurts, and we can invite God into the spaces where our family failed to show up.

Because even when family fractures, *our need to be loved remains the same*. Our Creator—our true Father—is still able to meet that need in ways no earthly structure ever could.

# Chapter 4 Reflection Questions: Whole or Fractured? Who Gets to Decide?

1. What unspoken pain have you carried from your family structure—blended, broken, or both?
   Are there stories or dynamics you've tried to forget, but they still impact you today?

2. In what ways did silence or favoritism shape your sense of belonging or identity?
   How did it affect the way you saw yourself in relation to others?

3. What conversations do you wish had happened? If you could go back and say one thing to bring clarity or healing, what would it be?

4. Ask God to reveal where He was in the midst of the fracture. Write a prayer for healing for yourself and for those who may have hurt you, knowingly or unknowingly.

____________________________________________

____________________________________________

____________________________________________

____________________________________________

____________________________________________

# Chapter 5

## WHEN CULTURE MEETS COMMUNITY

What happens when culture meets community? More than language, food, fashion, or tradition, culture is the unspoken rhythm of a group of people. It's the heartbeat of a group that shares values, beliefs, customs, and an understanding of what matters, and when those values are aligned, something powerful happens: a true *community* is born.

But here's the tension: not every group of people gathered together is a community. Some are simply coexisting. Sharing space but not spirit. Attending the same events but not carrying the same convictions. Walking in parallel but not in purpose.

We often assume that proximity equals belonging, but that couldn't be further from the truth. Just because people look like you, live near you, or speak the same language doesn't mean you share the same values or vision. Without intentional alignment, a common foundation of identity, purpose, and belief, you don't have a community. You have a crowd.

The danger of existing in a crowd that *feels* like community but lacks true connection is that it will eventually leave you empty. You'll keep showing up, keep serving, keep participating. But underneath it all, you'll still feel unknown, unseen, and unfulfilled.

That's why we have to ask ourselves hard questions:

- Am I part of a culture that reflects what I believe in and who I want to become?
- Do the people I surround myself with share a vision for growth, healing, and accountability?
- Or have I settled for comfortable routines with people who only mirror familiarity, not faith?

True community challenges you *and* covers you. It sees you *and* holds you accountable.

It's not built on trends, it's built on trust, shared truth, and spiritual alignment. When culture and community walk hand in hand, something sacred is formed. That's what the early church was in Acts. That's what Jesus modeled with His disciples, and that's what God still calls us to pursue today.

So here's the real question: Are you connected to a culture that nurtures your identity in Christ, or are you just passing time with people who look the part but don't share the heart?

My senior year of high school was a true turning point. Up until then, I had checked all the boxes: good grades, active in the community, respected by peers. I was a student who was well-integrated, embraced my culture, and understood what it meant to be part of something bigger than myself. At least, that's what it looked like from the outside.

Inside, I felt lost. It was like I was chasing something I couldn't name, an undefined longing to belong somewhere deeper. I struggled with acceptance, not because people excluded me, but because I didn't really understand what *belonging* meant. It wasn't about being in the room, it was about being *seen*. While I was often in the center of things, I still felt invisible.

I remained a virgin throughout high school, a choice rooted in my values and my faith. But I didn't wear that as a badge. If anything, I carried it as a question: *Why does this make me feel so different?*

I loved basketball, and I wore it like a uniform: baggy clothes, gym attire, athletic energy. But I hated being mistaken for "one of the guys." I longed to be seen as a young woman, not just "The Homey" or "Lil Sis." I wanted to be noticed, not for what I did, but for who I was.

Yet, how could they see that side of me when I had buried it under layers of performance, clothing, and confusion? That season of my life was full of contradictions. I was confident but insecure, accepted but misunderstood, outwardly celebrated but inwardly questioning who I truly was.

I didn't realize it then, but I had started to submit to a culture that was never truly mine. I bought into the idea that being seen meant being chosen sexually. That womanhood meant being desired. That belonging meant blending in, even if that meant losing parts of myself in the process.

By the time I reached my sophomore year of college, I lost my virginity, not because I had come into a deep understanding of love or connection, but because I was still chasing that same desire: *See me. Want me. Choose me.*

But I wasn't choosing *myself.* I had embraced a false community, one built on imitation and insecurity. A culture that told me what I had to look like, dress like, and act like to be valuable. A community that applauded sameness but made no room for sacred difference. In all of that, God's grace met me.

Even in moments where I made decisions outside of His will, His mercy didn't abandon me. He brought *His* culture into my broken culture. He cast His shadow over my inconsistency, covering my shame with compassion, and showing me that I still belonged to *Him*—even when I didn't feel like I belonged to myself.

That's what makes God's community different. It's not built on popularity or performance. It's built on presence. He doesn't need you to perform to belong. He just wants you close enough to reflect Him again.

It's not just about the culture of the community, it's about character of the community as well. It's about walking with people who call out your identity, not just your potential. Who reflect the heart of God back to you when your own reflection has grown blurry.

This is the community I craved. The culture I didn't even know I needed. A culture that reminds me of a simple but powerful truth: you don't have to become something to belong to God. You already belong, you just have to come home.

For so long, I thought belonging was about performance, proving I was worthy of love, acceptance, and space. But the Kingdom isn't like that. Kingdom community is rooted not in what you do, but in *who you are*: a child of God. When I reflect on Scripture, there's one story that illustrates this so clearly: the story of Moses.

When we think about Moses, we often jump to the "big" moments: the parting of the Red Sea, the plagues of Egypt, the Ten Commandments. Or we skip ahead to the part where he realizes he's Hebrew and becomes the deliverer of God's people. But between those moments is a long, complicated journey—a journey of identity.

Moses was born into a time of great oppression. Pharaoh had ordered every Hebrew baby boy to be killed, fearing the growth and strength of the Israelite people. His mother, desperate to save him, placed him in a basket and sent him down the Nile River. He was discovered and adopted by Pharaoh's daughter and raised as Egyptian royalty (Exodus 2:1-10).

From the outside, Moses had every privilege: wealth, power, education. But deep inside, there was a conflict he couldn't yet name. He wasn't Egyptian, not truly. He didn't grow up fully Hebrew either. His life was a constant tension between two worlds, one that nurtured him and one that birthed him.

As he grew, this internal conflict boiled over. When he saw an Egyptian beating a Hebrew slave, Moses' hidden identity erupted in anger. He killed the Egyptian and fled to Midian (Exodus 2:11-15). This wasn't just a physical escape, it was an emotional and spiritual exile. He was running not only from Pharaoh but from the confusion of who he was.

In Midian, Moses became a shepherd. It's easy to overlook this chapter in his life, but this season was critical. For 40 years, Moses lived away from both the Egyptian palace and the Hebrew slaves. He wasn't living out a grand calling. He was tending sheep, marrying, raising a family, and, most importantly, being stripped of everything he thought defined him.

Then came the moment that changed everything: the burning bush (Exodus 3:1-6). God revealed Himself to Moses, calling him by name and declaring, "I have chosen you to deliver My people." Moses resisted. He doubted. He said, "Who am I that I should go to Pharaoh and bring the Israelites out of Egypt?" (Exodus 3:11).

This is the gap we often overlook, the place between knowing who you *are* and accepting what God says you *can be*. Moses knew the facts of his identity, he was Hebrew by blood and Egyptian by upbringing, but he hadn't yet embraced the calling that would redefine his life.

Moses' story is one of culture meeting community. For years, he was caught between two cultures, unsure where he belonged. But when God called him, his identity and purpose became clear, not because of where he was raised, but because of who he was created to be.

This resonates with me so deeply because I've lived that tension. I've craved community, but I've tried to fit into cultures that didn't reflect who I truly was. I've mistaken activity for belonging, thinking I had to "become" something to earn my place. But Moses' life reminds us that our identity doesn't come from the culture we're born into or the one we've adopted, it comes from God's call over us.

# Chapter 5 Reflection Questions: "The Culture I Carried"

1. Have you ever felt surrounded, but still alone?
   What spaces in your life gave the appearance of community but left you feeling empty?

2. In what ways did you change or compromise yourself to feel seen or accepted?
   Were those changes rooted in truth, or insecurity?

3. What false cultural beliefs have shaped your view of womanhood or identity?
   How has God redefined those for you?

4. Write a letter to your younger self.
   Speak to her/him as someone who now understands what true belonging and identity in Christ looks like. Let them know you were always seen.

Chapter 6

# WHEN BELONGING BREAKS DOWN

There's a common phrase many of us hear and maybe even say: *"I don't need anyone. I can do this all by myself."*

But if we're honest, deep down, we know that's not true.

From the very beginning of time, God showed us that we were created *to belong*. After forming Adam from the dust and breathing life into him, God made a declaration: *"It is not good for man to be alone."* From Adam's rib, He created woman, not just as a companion, but as a *help mate*. This wasn't just about marriage, it was about relationship. It was about connection. It was about belonging.

Belonging is in our DNA. We were designed not only to reflect God but to dwell in healthy relationship with Him and with one another. So when we deny that truth, or try to operate outside of it, we begin to malfunction. Our souls struggle. Our choices reflect confusion. Our identity suffers.

That's exactly what happened to me. My first experience with sexual intimacy wasn't rooted in love or covenant, it was rooted in broken belonging. I didn't know it then, but I was trying to fill a void that was spiritually, emotionally, and identity based. That one moment opened the door to others, and I began to operate outside of God's will for relationships and connection.

I wasn't trying to be rebellious. I was trying to belong. But instead of walking in the belonging that was already mine in Christ, I pursued imitation communities and counterfeit love. The more I searched for fulfillment in people, the emptier I became. With every connection that pulled me further from God's will, the further I felt from *myself.*

Eventually, I hit the bottom. Not because God left me, but because I had built so many versions of belonging that He was never part of to begin with. The weight of false identity finally broke me open.

That's when I surrendered. I came to a place where it was no longer about relationships, approval, or social acceptance. It became about *me and God.* Although that wasn't my initial desire, it became the foundation of my healing. When I surrendered, He became *enough.* When I prioritized Him, He added what was necessary. But only after I realigned my posture.

Matthew 6:33 became my anchor:

*"But seek first the kingdom of God and His righteousness, and all these things will be added to you."*

We quote it often, but do we live it? We are a generation that struggles with order and prioritization. We give parts of ourselves to people, places, and things that were never designed to carry us. We let emotions and culture define our values, and then wonder why we feel so far from God.

But His Word is clear.

*"If you love me, keep my commandments."* (John 14:15)

*"Not everyone who says to me, 'Lord, Lord,' will enter the kingdom of heaven... then I will tell them plainly, 'I never knew you. Depart from me.'"* (Matthew 7:21–23)

Those verses aren't about condemnation, they're about alignment. God isn't looking for performance. He's looking for posture. It is possible to *look* like you belong while your heart is miles away. But when we finally stop running, striving, and hiding, and come back to Him, we find the belonging we were always searching for; not in people, not in performance, but in Him.

The story of Jonah is a perfect reflection of that journey. In the Book of Jonah, we meet a prophet with a calling straight from God. His assignment was clear: *"Go to the great city of Nineveh and preach against it, because its wickedness has come up before me."* (Jonah 1:2) Instead of obeying, Jonah ran. Not because he was incapable, but because he was unwilling. He boarded a ship going in the complete opposite direction of where God told him to go.

Sound familiar? Jonah's reaction wasn't about confusion. It was about resistance. He knew exactly what God said, but he didn't like it. It didn't fit his personal preferences or his comfort. So instead of embracing the call, he chose escape, and how often do we do the same?

We say things like:

- "That can't be for me."
- "Surely God doesn't expect me to do that."
- "Maybe He meant that for someone else."

But deep down, we know we've heard His voice. We know He's stirred something within us. Still, we run.

Jonah's attempt to flee wasn't harmless. It created chaos, not just for himself, but for everyone around him. The storm God sent wasn't just about Jonah's disobedience; it was a wake-up call. A signal that you can't escape divine purpose, not without consequences.

When the sailors realized the storm was Jonah's doing, they tried everything to save him. But eventually, Jonah had to confront the truth. *"Pick me up and throw me into the sea,"* he said. *"And it will become calm."* (Jonah 1:12) It's a powerful moment of accountability.

Jonah stopped running.

And in that moment—right in the middle of the sea— God provided a space for transformation. The great fish wasn't punishment, it was preservation and it was grace.

Inside the belly of that fish, Jonah had no distractions, no excuses, and nowhere else to go. All he could do was surrender, and he did.

*"In my distress I called to the Lord, and He answered me… When my life was ebbing away, I remembered You, Lord."* (Jonah 2:2,7)

After three days in the depths, Jonah was spit out onto dry land. He was not the same man who had run from God, but one who had been reshaped by mercy. If we're honest, there's a lot of Jonah in all of us.

God gives us assignments, speaks to us through His Word, confirms His will in subtle and obvious ways, and yet, we run. Not always physically. Sometimes it's emotionally and spiritually. We distract ourselves, immerse ourselves in busyness, convince ourselves that our way is better, safer, or easier.

But eventually, we hit a storm. Eventually, we find ourselves in a place that looks like rock bottom, but is actually God's classroom. Not to condemn us, but to realign us.

To remind us of who we are and what we've been created to do.

The real question isn't, "Why did God take me through this?" It's, "Why did I resist His way in the first place?" We must confront the truth: it wasn't Him. It was us.

We stepped outside of His will. We delayed obedience. We doubted His wisdom and trusted our fear, and yet, He still welcomes us back.

That's what grace looks like.

The world tells us belonging is about approval and acceptance. But in the Kingdom, belonging begins at *surrender.* Jonah belonged to God long before he obeyed Him. You and I belong to God long before we "get it right." When we finally return to the One who called us, when we stop pretending, running, performing, we realize He never left.

# Chapter 6 Reflection Questions: Realigning Belonging

5. Where have you searched for belonging that left you feeling more broken than before? What relationships or choices pulled you further from God's will?

6. Have you ever mistaken acceptance from people as affirmation from God?
What's the difference?

7. Write a prayer of realignment. Confess where you misplaced your belonging and invite God to restore your identity and order your life with Him at the center.

# Chapter 7

# CREATED FOR KINGDOM CONNECTION

From the beginning, creation was God's way of showing us His intention not only for the earth, but for *us*. He painted a picture of order, love, safety, stability, and spiritual health. He didn't just create man and woman, He created *family*. That first union in Eden wasn't only about companionship; it was about covenant and legacy.

It took me a while to understand that. For years, I searched. I reached. I made decisions that were outside of God's will. I confused love with attention and belonging with availability. I saw my past as disqualifying me from the future God could have for me. Then, I surrendered. When I finally stopped searching and fully gave my heart back to God, something shifted; not just in my spirit, but in my entire life.

For years, the early part of my adult journey was marked by cycles of pain and confusion. I joined the Army looking for purpose and structure, but instead I found myself in one unhealthy relationship after another. I clung to the idea of love, needing it, chasing it, believing that if I just tried harder, gave more, or stayed longer, something would change.

I made a commitment to a man outside the covenant of marriage, and in doing so, I made a covenant with heartbreak. I became emotionally entangled in a version of love that wasn't built to last, and it began to destroy parts of me. But I stayed. I convinced myself that if I was just a better girlfriend, maybe even a future wife, it would all be worth it.

But deep down, I knew something was off. That mentality wasn't aligned with God's purpose for my life. I was settling for the familiar pain instead of reaching for the promised peace. It took one heartbreak too many for me to finally look up and cry out from the depths of my soul: "Lord, I'm tired of doing it my way. Please, show me Yours."

That prayer became a turning point. About nine months later, I met my husband. The way we met wasn't ideal, certainly not how I imagined God would write my love story. But that's the beauty of grace: it doesn't always enter through the door you expect. It slips in quietly, tenderly, and sometimes unexpectedly.

At the time, I couldn't see it for what it was. But my husband, Joel, could. He had a clarity I hadn't yet walked in. While I was still questioning, Joel was already trusting. He recognized the divine fingerprints on our meeting. He saw the assignment before I even realized there was one.

At first, I resisted. After all the emotional wreckage I'd survived, I had grown protective of my space with God. I finally found comfort in the secret place, and I was afraid of confusing another emotional connection for divine confirmation. I didn't want to step outside of that sacred space too soon. My past had conditioned me to associate love with delay and pain. I felt like the children of Israel, wandering through my own desert, thinking I had to earn restoration by suffering long enough.

But here's what I forgot: God's grace doesn't operate on human timelines.

Joel reminded me of something I needed to reclaim:

*"He who finds a wife finds a good thing and obtains favor from the Lord."* (Proverbs 18:22)

I wasn't being pulled away from God. I was being pursued according to His promise. For the first time in my life, I wasn't searching, I was found. Not just by a man, but by a promise. By a love that was rooted in Kingdom order. By a covering that reflected the Father's heart for me.

Our courtship was brief—six months from introduction to "I do." We married and immediately moved thousands of miles away from family, starting our life together in Anchorage, Alaska. It was beautiful. It was terrifying. It was one of the hardest seasons of our lives and our marriage.

Everything was unfamiliar. The landscape was cold. The isolation was real. The adjustments were overwhelming.

But in that unfamiliar place, we discovered something priceless: We had God, and we had each other. There were no safety nets, no distractions, no shortcuts. Just two people, joined in covenant, learning how to trust God not only individually but as one.

That season taught me that sometimes, God has to remove you from everything familiar to show you what is foundational. That real love isn't built on history, convenience, or emotional highs. It's built on covenant, obedience, presence and surrender.

In that place, in the middle of the unfamiliar, I didn't just find love, I found wholeness. I found peace. I found me. That was the beginning. *His* beginning, not ours.

It mirrored Eden in a way. Adam and Eve had no crowd, no blueprint, no family tree to lean on. They had each other and the presence of God. While our circumstances weren't identical, the spiritual reality was the same: the foundation of our union was not built on culture, tradition, or convenience. It was built on covenant.

When we lose sight of God's original intention for us, the image we bear begins to blur. We start to reflect culture more than Christ, performance more than purpose, self more than Spirit. But when we return to God's design through surrender, obedience, and alignment we begin to look like Him again. Our reflection becomes clearer. Our relationships become healthier. Our purpose becomes undeniable.

Fourteen years later, I can look at my life and say with confidence: this is not the world's doing. This is *God's grace*.

Joel and I now have three beautiful daughters: Journey, Joy, and Janelle. They are not just our children, they are reflections of God's affection, compassion, creativity, and love toward us. We are a family of five, not by accident but by *divine grace*. Our daughters are living proof that God can take broken beginnings and build a Kingdom legacy.

We are no longer just image bearers, we are legacy builders. Our legacy is not built on perfection. It's built on *presence*. His presence.

We are here today because of it, and it is our prayer that the image we bear today—the image of our loving, faithful, redemptive Father—will be passed on to our children, and their children, until every generation knows:

*This is what grace looks like. This is what love built. This is what legacy reflects. Kingdom connection.*

# Chapter 7 Reflection Questions:
# Kingdom Connection

1. In what areas of your life have you been "doing it your way"? What patterns, relationships, or decisions have you made outside of God's will that you now see need surrender?

2. Have you mistaken emotional connection for divine confirmation in relationships or friendships? How can you begin to discern the difference?

3. What does it look like to be "found by a promise" instead of striving to create your own version of love or purpose?

4. How has your past conditioned your expectations for love, healing, or trust?
Are there any lies you've believed about your worth because of your past experiences?

5. Where is God currently asking you to trust Him, even if the environment feels cold, unfamiliar, or uncomfortable? What might He be building in you through this season?

6. Write a letter to God surrendering one specific area of your life (relationships, control, shame, fear) that you've held onto too tightly. Be honest. Be raw. Then ask Him to show you His plan in that area.

# Chapter 8

## BUILDING KINGDOM COMMUNITY

The greatest joy of my life has been experiencing the comfort, companionship, and guidance of the Holy Spirit *here*, in real time, on this side of eternity. His presence has been more than a theological concept to me; it's been an anchor in every season. But one of the hardest truths I've come to accept is this:

There is a lot of *confusion* in what we call the Kingdom community. We often equate Kingdom with church attendance. We assume that just because we show up, serve on a ministry, or attend events, we're a part of something meaningful. But if we're honest—brutally honest—we don't even *like* most of the people we go to church with. We rarely do life with them outside the church walls. We don't know their struggles, their stories, or even their real names beyond Sunday introductions.

What kind of community is that? It certainly doesn't resemble *Kingdom*.

For over 21 years in the Army, I've served under the spiritual care of many churches. Each duty station brought new opportunities, new partnerships with leaders, and new environments that exposed me to a different way of looking at Kingdom. In the early years of my adult life before marriage, I often sought out churches that resembled what I had experienced growing up, places filled with activity, rhythm, and a familiar church culture.

Looking back, I now recognize that much of what I experienced in my early church life was more of a performance of community than the power of Kingdom. It looked like Kingdom. We had the songs, the sermons, the events, the altar calls. But transformation was shallow.

We gathered, but we weren't always growing. We participated, but we weren't always surrendering. We were present, but not always postured. Instead of being built into mature believers, many of us were cycling through religious tradition. Sunday after Sunday, doing what we had always done, checking spiritual boxes while quietly starving for deeper connection.

We were pursuing religion over relationship. We honored God with routine but not always with reverence. I didn't even realize how much I was missing until God disrupted the pattern. That disruption came when my husband Joel and I moved to Anchorage, Alaska. It wasn't just another military assignment. It was a spiritual interruption. There, we were led to New Season Christian Church. The name wasn't accidental, it was confirmation.

"See, I am doing a new thing! Now it springs up; do you not perceive it?" — Isaiah 43:19

New Season was exactly that, a new beginning. Not just for where we worshiped, but for how we worshiped. For the first time in a long time, we weren't just attending church, we were being shaped by it, called into accountability, invited into deeper service. We were stretched beyond comfort. We weren't just doing church, we were becoming the Church.

That moment established a pattern that would follow us in each transition of our military career. After 3 years in Anchorage, Alaska, we transitioned to San Antonio, Texas, where we were led to Covenant Life Church. In this space, the emphasis shifted. It wasn't just about passion, it was about perseverance.

"Let us hold unswervingly to the hope we profess, for He who promised is faithful." — Hebrews 10:23

Covenant Life taught us something foundational: spiritual maturity is not measured by excitement, it is measured by endurance. It is revealed in faithfulness when obedience feels heavy. It is proven in commitment when convenience disappears. We learned that growth in Christ requires staying power. Not emotional highs, not seasonal zeal, but rooted consistency. Covenant is not built on feelings; it is sustained by faithfulness.

From there, our next assignment led us to Kingdom Life, and something shifted. There was an intentional pursuit of Kingdom relationships that was evident in the fruit of that ministry. Community was not treated as optional; it was cultivated. Values were not assumed; they were protected. Their emphasis on placing the Kingdom first was not just preached, it was practiced. That emphasis created the shift in perspective we didn't even realize we needed.

This was during the post-COVID phase, when isolation had quietly fractured what once felt like strong community. What had once resembled vibrant Kingdom fellowship in many places had become fragments, separated, cautious, disconnected. Fear and fatigue had threatened unity. Proximity had been replaced with distance.

## But Kingdom Life was intentional.

Intentional about preserving righteousness. Intentional about protecting unity. Intentional about restoring spiritual hunger. It was clear they were operating from a Kingdom perspective, not a survival perspective.

"But seek ye first the Kingdom of God and His righteousness…" — Matthew 6:33

That scripture became more than a verse; it became a lens. We began to understand that we were not simply church attendees occupying seats. We were ambassadors representing eternity. Our lives were meant to reflect more than participation; they were meant to reflect authority, alignment, and Kingdom assignment.

**Attendance was no longer the goal, alignment was. Presence was no longer enough, pursuit was required.** Kingdom Life helped us see that true community is sustained when righteousness is prioritized, when relationships are rooted in Christ, and when every gathering is centered on advancing His rule, not our comfort.

That realization deepened us. Finally, we arrived at Christ the Healer Church. This season was different. It didn't just resemble growth, it felt like activation. Everything we had learned in previous seasons converged. The devotion from New Season. The commitment from Covenant Life. The identity from Kingdom Life.

Now, it was time to walk in it. "For the kingdom of God is not a matter of talk but of power." — 1 Corinthians 4:20

This was no longer about learning principles. It was about living them. At Christ the Healer, God revealed a blueprint for what authentic Kingdom community looks like: transparency, accountability, compassion, correction, and presence. Not perfection, but alignment.

True community is not built on programs or impressive worship teams. It is built on the presence of God dwelling among people who are submitted to Him. You can't manufacture that. You can't substitute performance for presence and expect transformation. Here's what I began to understand: the enemy's strategy is not always chaos. Sometimes it's comfort.

Cycles without growth.

Activity without intimacy.

Routine without revelation.

He doesn't mind if we attend church. He fears when we surrender. The greatest danger is not sin alone, it is separation.

Separation doesn't always look rebellious. Sometimes it looks religious.

That realization forced me to examine my own heart. Was I serving from reverence or familiarity? Was I worshiping from awe or habit? Was I building Kingdom or maintaining comfort?

For most of my life, I knew there was a God. I honored Him. I acknowledged Him. I served Him. But this season taught me the difference between honoring God and reverencing Him.

Honor can be verbal. Reverence is positional. It is when your heart bows low. When your will yields. When your routine becomes surrendered. We have become comfortable with holy things.

We sing familiar songs. We quote familiar scriptures.

We attend familiar services.

But familiarity without reverence leads to stagnation. When reverence returns, everything shifts. **The same worship feels different. The same prayers feel deeper. The same church feels alive.** Because when your "how" is rooted in obedience, and your "who" includes the presence of God, the routine becomes refined. The ordinary becomes anointed, and what looks the same becomes supernatural. Transition taught me something powerful:

**Every church was preparation.**

**Every pastor was instruction.**

**Every move was divine sequencing.**

Nothing was wasted, and nothing was random. We were being built, and now I understand this clearly:

Kingdom community is not about finding the perfect place. It is about becoming the right person aligned with your God given assignment. We all struggle with this at some point, but healing comes with admittance and movement in a different direction—His Direction

When you are submitted to God, He will order your steps, even your spiritual ones. He will lead you to the places that grow you. He will move you when it is time to stretch. He will anchor you when it is time to build.

When reverence enters your life, routine becomes revelation. Your church attendance becomes discipleship. Your worship becomes surrender. Your life becomes holy ground.

# Chapter 8 Reflection Questions: Redefining Community

1. When you reflect on your church history, were you growing or simply attending?
   What evidence supports your answer?

2. Think about the spiritual "seasons" you've experienced. What did each season teach you about devotion, commitment, or identity?

3. Have you resisted a spiritual transition because it felt uncomfortable or unfamiliar? What might God have been trying to develop in you during that shift?

4. Are you currently planted in a community that stretches you spiritually or one that keeps you comfortable?

5. Are you building your faith on programs and personalities or on personal relationship with God?

6. Do your routines create space for revelation or are they filled with repetition without reflection?

7. What would it look like for you to move from being a consumer of church to becoming a contributor to the Kingdom?

<h1 style="text-align:center">Chapter 9</h1>

# THE SAME BUT DIFFERENT – THE IDENTITY WE SHARE

We began this journey at the starting place. In Chapter 1, we stood face-to-face with our mirrors: our beginnings, our questions, our inherited narratives. We wrestled with where we started and whether our start determined our future.

But we learned something powerful: Your starting place explains you. It does not define you.

In Chapter 2, we returned to the foundation:

**We were made in His image.**

Before culture shaped us.

Before family influenced us.

Before pain fractured us.

We were formed by the hands of the Potter.

"We are the clay, You are the potter; we are all the work of Your hand." — Isaiah 64:8

That truth anchors everything because if we are made in His image, then identity is not something we invent is something we uncover.

## Nature vs. Nurture

In Chapter 3, we confronted the human dilemma.

Nature gives us design.

Nurture gives us exposure.

Some of us were nurtured in stability.

Others were raised in survival.

But the tension between nature and nurture does not cancel the image of God. It only complicates how we discover it.

We learned that while we may not choose our environment, we always choose our alignment. And that choice determines whether we repeat patterns—or break them.

## Whole or Fractured?

In Chapter 4, we asked the uncomfortable question:

Who gets to decide if we are whole or fractured?

The world defines wholeness by perfection. God defines wholeness by surrender.

We realized that fractures do not disqualify us, they invite us to return to the One who restores.

Because in a fallen world, we will all be exposed to brokenness.

But we are not required to remain shaped by it.

## Community and Culture

In Chapter 5, we examined how community and culture influence identity. Culture shapes behavior.

Community shapes belonging.

But when culture drifts from Kingdom values, belonging becomes performance. We discovered that we can exist in a group and still feel unseen.

We can share space and still lack connection. Because true community is not proximity.

## It is shared pursuit.

## When Belonging Breaks Down

In Chapter 6, we faced the reality that belonging can fracture.

When we search for acceptance outside of God's will, we often mistake attachment for alignment.

We try to fill identity gaps with relationships, performance, or achievement.

But broken belonging reveals a deeper truth:

We were never meant to find identity horizontally before we secured it vertically. Belonging begins with the Father.

## Created for Kingdom Connection

In Chapter 7, we rediscovered design. We were not created for isolation.

From the very beginning, God said: "It is not good for man to be alone." Kingdom connection is not optional, it is foundational.

But connection without Christ becomes dependency. Connection rooted in Christ becomes covenant. We learned that we are the same in design—but different in assignment.

## Building Kingdom Community

In Chapter 8, we transitioned from church attendance to Kingdom alignment. We saw the difference between performance and presence. Between routine and reverence. Between gathering and growing.

We realized that Kingdom community is not about preference, it is about purpose. And that when our how is rooted in obedience and our who includes the presence of God…The ordinary becomes anointed.

## Bringing It All Together

So what does this mean for us?

It means:

*You may have started in brokenness, but you were formed in purpose.*

*You may have been nurtured in chaos, but you were created in order.*

*You may have felt fractured, but you were fashioned by perfect hands.*

*You may have struggled with belonging, but you were always called home.*

*We were all crafted by the same Creator.*

*We share the same breath.*

*The same divine imprint.*

But our stories unfold differently.

That is the beauty of being **The Same but Different.**

Different families.

Different exposures.

Different journeys.

But one Father.

One image.

One Kingdom.

## The Final Invitation

You cannot change where you started.

But you can decide who shapes you next.

Will you allow the world to continue defining you?

Or will you return to the Potter?

Because here is the truth: Identity is not achieved.

It is received. Wholeness is not performed.

It is surrendered to.

Community is not consumed.

It is cultivated.

Legacy is not accidental.

It is intentional.

## Final Reflection

You are not a mistake.

You are not too far gone.

You are not defined by what fractured you.

You are the intentional handiwork of God.

Before the world labeled you,

He named you.

Before culture shaped you,

He formed you.

Before you wandered,

He called you.

And He is still calling.

Calling you to return.

Calling you to reflect Him.

Calling you to build Kingdom community rooted in truth.

Calling you to embrace the authenticity of His creation—

# Me.You.Us.

You are different by design. But you are the same in divine destiny. So, rise and let the world witness the image of the One who created you—

Reflected.

Redeemed.

Fully alive in Christ.

Fashioned by the same Father.

Entrusted with a unique assignment.

Beginning again—not from your past,

But from His purpose.

This is not just the end of a book. It is the start of ownership. It starts with surrender. It continues with reverence.

And it is sustained through Kingdom connection.

**You were made for this. Now walk in it. And enjoy the journey.**

**Prayer of Returning:**

My Father, My God,

Today, I return.

Not just to a belief system, but to the beginning.

To *You*, my Creator,

The One who formed me with intention,

Who knew me before I took my first breath,

And who has never stopped calling me home.

I let go of every false label.

Every distorted mirror.

Every lie whispered by the enemy or spoken from my own lips.

The moments I convinced myself I was too broken, too different, or too far gone to be redeemed.

Today, I renounce those lies.

And I declare: **I am Yours.**

I was made in Your image.

I carry the same breath You breathed into Adam,

And I choose now to walk in alignment with the identity You authored for my life—

Not the one the world tried to assign.

I reunite with You, not just to *know* You,

But to *know myself in You*.

To see my life as a reflection of Your love,

Your compassion,

Your grace, poured out from generation to generation.

I embrace my authentic self:

Not the version shaped by trauma, performance, or people-pleasing.

But the one born with eternal purpose.

The one You created to reflect Your light in the earth.

No longer will I shrink back.

No longer will I conform to the patterns of this world.

No longer will I search for belonging in places that never meant to hold me.

**My belonging is in You.**

**My identity is secure.**

**My future is Kingdom-aligned.**

This is not the end.

It is the beginning.

And I walk forward,

Fully seen.

Fully known.

Fully loved.

In Jesus' mighty name,

**Amen.**

## Scriptures of Foundation

### Acts 3:19 (NIV)

"Repent, then, and turn to God, so that your sins may be wiped out, that times of refreshing may come from the Lord."

### Romans 10:9 (NIV)

"If you declare with your mouth, 'Jesus is Lord,' and believe in your heart that God raised Him from the dead, you will be saved."

# Conclusion

## EMBRACING THE AUTHENTICITY OF GOD'S CREATION – ME, YOU, US

We've traveled through chapters of difference, identity, culture, and truth.

We've peeled back the layers of our past, our pain, and our perceptions.

And now we arrive here, at the place of **authenticity.**

Because this journey was never just about understanding *me.*

It was about understanding *you.*

Ultimately, about discovering the beauty of **us**—the collective creation of a loving God.

Yes, we're different.

Different families. Different struggles. Different starting points.

But we were all shaped by the same hands.

Breathed into by the same Spirit.

Set apart by the same Father.

When God created humanity, He didn't make copies—He made reflections.

Each one bearing a unique imprint of His nature.

Each one carrying value, purpose, and identity.

## Not in isolation. But in community.

The world may try to divide us by race, by gender, by economics, by labels and lifestyles.

But the truth is, we are all invited to return—to wholeness, to identity, to Him.

To embrace who we really are: **authentic, created, chosen.**

So, as you turn the final page, ask yourself:

- What have I believed about *me* that God never said?
- What judgments have I made about *you* that God never endorsed?
- What barriers have I placed between *us* that God never designed?

Because this is the moment we stop just seeing differences and start **celebrating design**. This is where we let go of performance and step into purpose. This is where we begin to **reflect the image of God in every space we enter—together.**

So here's the call:

Embrace the authenticity of God's creation.

Embrace the unique way He shaped *you*.

Honor the divine design in *others*.

And let us, *together*, reflect the unity, diversity, and beauty of **His Kingdom**.

This is not just a conclusion.

This is your new beginning.

**Me. You. Us.**

**Different on purpose.**

**Same by design.**

**One in Christ.**

So here are a few things to consider as you close this book and walk forward into the life God designed for you:

## 1. Identity is a Gift, Not an Achievement

You don't have to *earn* the image of God—you were *born* into it. Your job is not to create identity; it's to **uncover** the identity He already placed in you.

## 2. Experiences Don't Define You—God Does

Yes, your upbringing, pain, trauma, and past have shaped you. But they don't get the final say. God has the power to use even the most broken beginnings to build something beautiful.

## 3. Surrender is the Key to Clarity

The more you try to find yourself through the world, the more lost you'll feel. True clarity comes when you lay down your need to be accepted by everyone else and pick up the truth of who you are in *Him*.

## 4. Community Matters—But it Starts With God

Don't settle for performance-based religion or shallow relationships. Seek Kingdom community. Surround yourself with people who love like Jesus and push you to reflect Him more and more each day.

## 5. Your Legacy Starts With Ownership

You can't pass down what you don't own. Own your identity in Christ. Let your children, your community, and your world see what it means to walk confidently in the image of God. Let your life preach what your words cannot.

## Final Reflection

You are not a mistake.

You are not too far gone.

You are not forgotten, forsaken, or overlooked.

You are the intentional handiwork of a loving and all-knowing Creator. He formed you **on purpose**, with **purpose**, and for **purpose**. Before the world gave you names, labels, or limitations, God called you **His**.

The journey you've walked—no matter how fractured, delayed, or detoured—has never disqualified you from belonging. In fact, it's in those very places of brokenness that God's restoration shines brightest. Your scars don't disprove your worth. They prove His power to redeem.

Every single day you wake up is another opportunity to reflect His image more clearly. Not through perfection, but through **presence**. Not by striving to become someone else, but by surrendering to who you were created to be all along.

So live boldly.

Stand firmly.

Love freely.

Forgive often.

Grow intentionally.

Own your identity—not the one culture assigns, but the one Heaven has authored.

You are His image-bearer.

You are a light in a dark world.

You are the reflection of grace, mercy, and truth.

You don't need to earn God's love—it's already yours.

You don't need to chase belonging—you've already been chosen.

You don't have to prove your worth—He's already declared it.

So walk in it.

Speak from it.

Parent from it.

Build from it.

Heal from it.

You were created to reflect the very character of God—

Compassion.

Wisdom.

Joy.

Strength.

Righteousness.

Peace.

And above all, **love**.

You are **different by design**,

But you are the **same in divine destiny**.

So rise with confidence.

Shine with purpose.

And let the world witness the image of the One who created you—

## Reflected. Redeemed. Fully alive in Christ.

You were fashioned by the **same Father**,

Yet entrusted with a **unique assignment**—

One that only you can fulfill,

One that begins not tomorrow, but **today**.

Walk boldly.

Live freely.

Bear His likeness with joy.

And never forget:

You are the evidence of a Creator who makes no mistakes.

This is your moment.

This is your beginning.

## You were made for this. Enjoy The Journey........

# About the Author

**R**andalle Marie Cheron Carter is an ordained minister, Army veteran, and founder of *The Pursuit of Kingdom Ministries*—a Christ-centered movement dedicated to restoring spiritual, mental, and emotional wholeness. With over two decades of military service and more than ten years of ministerial leadership, Randalle blends discipline and compassion to guide others in discovering their identity in Christ.

She holds a Master's in Biblical Studies from the New Generation Full Gospel Institute and has faithfully served in both youth and adult ministries across the country. Her heart beats for discipleship, healing, and generational restoration—believing that freedom in Christ begins not just at the altar, but in the daily walk of surrender, obedience, and renewed perspective.

Randalle is not only a devoted wife to Joel Carter and loving mother to three beautiful daughters—Journey, Joy, and Janelle—but also a daughter, sister, aunt, friend, mentor, and most importantly, a beloved child of God. These many roles have shaped her unique approach to ministry, equipping her to connect with people across generations and life experiences. Whether through prayer, teaching, writing, or simply sitting in quiet counsel, she creates safe spaces where others can rediscover who they are and whose they are.

Her work continues to build Kingdom legacy by challenging readers to embrace their authentic selves as image bearers of God in a world that often distorts identity.

Though her voice remained quiet for many years, Randalle now speaks boldly—with a wisdom forged through trials and a love that flows straight from the heart of the Father. She is a champion of Kingdom connection, passionate about equipping others to walk in truth, live with purpose, and reflect the light of Christ in every space they enter.

Her greatest hope is simple but powerful: that you would come to know yourself through the One who created you and  walk confidently in the truth that you were never too far, never too lost, and never forgotten by God.

# Book Blurb

**The Same but Different**

*Embracing the Authenticity of God's Creation—Me, You, Us*

We were all created in the image of God—yet each of us carries a story shaped by pain, culture, family, and experience.

In *The Same but Different*, author and minister **Randalle Marie Cheron Carter** invites readers on a powerful journey of rediscovery—through broken beginnings, spiritual awakening, and the ongoing pursuit of wholeness in Christ. Drawing from her own life as a daughter, wife, mother, soldier, and disciple, Randalle weaves together vulnerability, biblical wisdom, and deep reflection to help readers reclaim the truth of who they are.

Whether you were raised in dysfunction or discipline, with abundance or absence, your identity is not determined by your past. It was formed by your Creator. Through the stories of Jacob, Jonah, Moses, the woman with the issue of blood, and Paul—intertwined with Randalle's own journey— this book reminds us that we may start from different places, but we all share the same divine destiny: to reflect God's image.

This is more than a memoir. It's a mirror. A reflection of the authentic self that can only be revealed in Christ. Inside these pages, you will be:

- Challenged to confront distorted versions of self-shaped by culture, trauma, and performance
- Encouraged to embrace spiritual identity rooted in God's Word and presence
- Equipped with journal prompts, declarations, and reflective questions to help you grow in spiritual clarity and confidence
- Invited to reunite with the Father through healing, surrender, and truth

If you've ever wrestled with identity, belonging, or believing you are enough, *The Same but Different* will speak to your soul. It's not about being perfect—it's about being present with the One who formed you. You are different by design. But you are the same in divine purpose.

Come home to who you really are.